T0196961

Learn
to Read
from Sounds

Florence Barnes

Order this book online at www.trafford.com
or email orders@trafford.com

Most Trafford titles are also available at major online book retailers.

Print information available on the last page.

ISBN: 978-1-4120-2050-3 (sc)
ISBN: 978-1-4122-2071-2 (e)

Library of Congress Control Number: 2012921703

Trafford rev. 08/24/2015

 www.trafford.com

North America & international
toll-free: 1 888 232 4444 (USA & Canada)
fax: 812 355 4082

"A solid grounding in sounds and letters ensures that children learn to read so that they can read to learn."

-   submitted to the Minster of Education for the Province of Manitoba by Parents Concerned About Standards in Education, January 24, 1994, in "Rhetoric Versus Reality."

"Literacy is the fundamental right of all citizens."

-   a working principle for the Task Force on Literacy, April 1989. Manitoba Government.

My purpose in writing this book is to promote the teaching of phonics to all children in schools.

Some teachers teach phonics well, but others do not. Some children learn to read well, but others do not. The problem is that there is no mandate given to educators to teach all children to read by teaching how the alphabet works in written language.

FACTS ABOUT PHONICS

An eight year old child struggles in the third grade unable to read and wonders what is wrong. One such tragedy is one too many, but it is repeated every year across North America. The reason is the refusal of the educational system to provide adequate teaching of letters and sounds.

We can choose to teach or not to teach the phonic system to children in school. When I say "teach", I mean just that, and not merely giving a little help here and there.

The only way to read words other than from sounds is to memorize words from how they look, or to guess using context to try to find a word that fits the meaning of what is being read. We write words the way we do for one reason only—that letters stand for the sounds of spoken language, so it makes sense to teach this system when we teach children to read.

Modern theorists do not agree as to how much phonics knowledge is necessary. They recommend some phonics along with other methods. "Some phonics" may mean that children know very little phonics.

A little phonics helps, but complete phonics knowledge is necessary for children to use it effectively in reading and spelling.

The "discovery" method of learning can be used in learning to read but we must not rely on children learning the letter sound system on their own. Too many children fail.

If children have a right to learn to read, they have a right to be taught to read. That is the job of the schools. Parents can help, but parents should not be blamed for their children's failure in learning to read when it is the teaching of reading that is missing.

The solution to the problem of teaching reading does not lie in a debate about whole language versus phonics. It lies in adding the teaching of complete and systematic phonics to whole language.

What is phonics?

Phonics is the representation of the sounds of spoken language by the letters of the alphabet.

What is whole language?

Whole language is a term used to describe ideas about learning language. It includes child-centered, experience-based, holistic learning. It came about as a movement to replace the sight word method of memorizing words, or "look and say". The sight word method had already replaced phonics as the way to teach children to read.

How do whole language theorists say that children should learn to read?

They say that children should learn to read by reading "whole texts" with "incidental" help from teachers who are sometime called "facilitators". Children are encouraged to use "strategies" such as sounding the first letters of words and guessing words from context.

They say that whole language is a philosophy of teaching and learning—not a method. Phonics is a method of teaching reading.

How is phonics helpful in reading and writing?

In reading, phonics enables us to read words from the sounds of the letters.

In spelling, phonics enables us to write words according to the sounds of the letters.

Does learning phonics require practice and drill?

Yes, practice and drill are required. Some children need more than others. Whole language activities can continue along with phonics instruction.

Does learning phonics produce slow readers?

A person reads slowly in the learning stage, when speed is not a priority. As with any new skill, speed increases with ability. Children learn to recognize words instantly, along with their phonics knowledge, so there is no reason to think they will read slowly because of phonics.

Is phonics difficult for children to learn?

Learning phonics is more difficult for some children than for others. This is the reason that some require more teaching than others. Groups or entire classes can be taught letters and sounds together in printing, spelling and reading lessons.

If children learn phonics, will they have trouble understanding what they read?

They will understand easily because they will be able to read the words easily. Children who can sound words can read any word, including those whose meanings they have not yet learned.

Does a teacher who teaches phonics have to give up whole language?

Teachers can add complete and systematic teaching of phonics to whole language. They can read to children, provide good books, give assistance as children try to read, and continue with any other whole language activities.

Are there too many rules in learning phonics?

There are rules to learn, but they can help in the process of learning to read. Learning phonics means learning how to read and write words from sounds—not just learning rules.

Is it harmful to teach sounds or words in isolation as some theorists claim?

Every letter and letter combination has its own sound or sounds when it is not connected with other letters. We can teach these sounds in isolation.

Although meanings of words become more clear as they are used in sentences and paragraphs, they do have meaning in isolation, and children should practice reading single words, as well as reading them in sentences and paragraphs.

What are reading skills?

Reading is a skill. If children can read words and understand them they can read. Understanding is not the problem. Children understand thousands of words before they begin school. What they have to learn is to tell what the printed words are. The basic skill needed is to know what the letters say.

Is learning to read words all there is to reading?

Opponents of phonics say that there is more to reading than just reading words. Of course there is. There is growth in comprehension, judgement, comparison and so on, but first it is necessary to have the ability to read the words.

Why is the phonic system not taught completely to all beginners in school?

Phonics is not taught completely to all beginners because of what people believe. Some whole language theorists believe that we should not teach phonics completely and systematically, and this belief is followed by many of those who are responsible for how children are taught.

Those who believe phonics must be taught, have not been able to convince the authorities of the need to reinstate complete phonics teaching in schools.

Who can change the system?

The Minister of Education can give the mandate to all teachers in the province to teach phonics to all children. The minister will then be speaking for parents, but will have to face the opposition of many members of the education bureaucracy who follow whole language policies. Many teachers would welcome the mandate to teach phonics. Teachers of the grades above primary would welcome the change of having all children in their classes able to read and spell. (A mandate may not be fair to some teachers who have graduated not learning phonics themselves. Extra training may be required.)

Parents' organizations are trying to bring back phonics teaching, but unless it is brought in as a policy in education, it is a long and difficult struggle.

Why is there opposition to teaching phonics?

Opponents of phonics give reasons for their opposition such as: phonics is too difficult; learning phonics is too boring;

children who learn phonics are slow readers; English is not a phonetic language; we must not teach sounds in isolation, and so on.

Educators say that phonics should be used as one of several methods of teaching reading. What is wrong with that?

There is nothing wrong with that as long as they make provision to teach children phonics properly so that they can use it as one method of learning to read. Using "some phonics" often means that children have very little phonics knowledge to use. If they know phonics they can use it along with any other methods there are.

What other methods are used in helping children learn to read?

We memorize words from sight, but those who do not know how to sound words from the letters that make up the words, have no alternative but to memorize them from how they look. Because there is no relation between how words look and their meanings, there is need for much repetition of memorized words in reading material.

Children who haven't learned to sound entire words may know the sounds of individual letters (which is a start in learning phonics) so they are encouraged to guess unknown words from their beginning sounds. Another strategy recommended is to see if there is a part of the word the same as a part of a word they already know, and from the known word they try to say that part in the new word. Because words have to make sense in the sentence or paragraph children are told to read ahead to see if the word they guessed fits the context. If it doesn't, they go back and try another guess, and finally if they are not successful they may be told to give up and skip the word and go on reading.

Do children learn to read by being read to?

Some children learn to read by being read to, but many do not. They have the advantage of experience and enjoyment, but there is no excuse for failing to teach every child to read and write.

Is it better for children to learn phonics on their own than to learn it from teaching?

Some theorists recommend "incidental" teaching only. Phonics is a tool to use in reading and writing. Children must acquire that tool as early as possible in school, so that they can use it, and improve it with use. Teaching phonics is more efficient than not teaching it, and loss of self-esteem due to reading failure will be prevented.

Was phonics taught in the past?

The "Oxford Companion to the English Language", states that in all schools in England during the industrial Revolution, children were drilled first on letter names and sounds, then on syllable and words.

Reading was taught from letters and sounds in North America also, until education authorities, rather than leaving well enough alone, introduced the sight word method.

Why did educators change from phonics to the sight word method?

Rudolf Flesch, in "Why Johnny Can't Read And What You Can Do About It" (1955) tells a story as related in an 1846 primer called the New Word Primer:

A teacher was sitting at the kitchen window of his boarding place watching the man of the house milking a cow out in the yard. He talked to a four year old girl sitting on his lap about what they saw. He noticed the word "cow" on a paper, pointed to it, and called the child's attention to the cow outside the window, and the sight word method was born! He began to teach reading words from sight, and against the protestations of parents who saw children were not learning to spell, this sight word method was adopted by the authorities.

Rudolf Flesch sees no reason why the author would make up this story, but whether it is true or not, this is about as much scientific basis as there is for memorizing words without knowledge of the sounds of the letters.

Rudolf Flesch says: "As soon as (this method) did start, trouble started too—the kind of trouble that is still with us more than a hundred years later." This author tried to convince authorities to bring back phonics in 1955, and again in 1981 in "Why Johnny Can't Read—A New Look At The Scandal Of Our Schools".

How did we get from the sight word method to whole language?

The sight word method was found to require reading material with poorly written stories because of the need to repeat words and to limit reading material to words memorized, so the next idea was that children would be able to learn to read on their own, with "incidental" help, as long as they were allowed to choose interesting books. The aim of whole language is to motivate children to want to learn to read, and to promote a love of reading and learning.

There is no provision to teach all children how to read and write words from sounds, so the tragedy of reading failure is the result.

Whole language theorists lump phonics and sight words together as a "bottom-up", "bits and pieces" method of learning to read. They prefer a "top down", whole text, meaning approach in which children get meaning from larger units of print without first learning how to read the words.

Educators claim that children are reading more than ever. Is this true?

Whole language policy encourages reading, so those children who can read are reading more. Those who do not learn to read well are not reading much.

If phonics is not being taught in the primary grades what can parents do?

Parents can try to promote the teaching of phonics individually or by joining groups. They can ask the Ministers of Education to reinstate phonics instruction. In the meantime children in school can not wait for reforms to happen. Most kindergarten teachers teach the sounds of the letters, so that is the first step. The next step is to teach blending of sounds together in words in writing, and sounding words in reading. If blending of sounds in words is not being taught in school, then children should learn it out of school.

Who can teach phonics?

Any person who knows phonics, and who is able to read can teach children to read and write from sounds.

How can we teach phonics?

Reading is the process of extracting meaning from written or printed language. Knowledge of phonics enables us to read the words, so that we can get meaning from print.

Some phonics is taught in most schools, but the amount varies from one class to another. Unless there is a policy to teach phonics to beginners completely and systematically, parents should supplement what children learn in school by a phonics program at home.

The phonic system is the same for everyone, regardless of the age of the learner. Young children can learn gradually, but for older children who have not learned phonics, a concentrated teaching program is needed.

We can talk to young children about the sounds at the beginnings of words. They learn the sounds of the language as they listen to and repeat rhymes and listen to stories and poems. Reading aloud to children is for enjoyment, but occasionally we can draw their attention to the sounds of the letters.

Children can begin to put letters together to make words by using letter cards cut from cardboard (cereal boxes).

As they try to read, we can help them to sound the words.

Children who are having difficulty learning to read may know the sounds of the letters but may not have learned to blend those sounds together in words. They may know the consonant sounds but may be unsure of the vowel sounds.

The outline on the following page may be used in a teaching program.

PHONICS

The sounds of the letters of the alphabet can be taught alone, and in words beginning with the sounds a – apple, b – box, c – cat.

The short vowel sounds are: a as in cat, e – hen, i – pig, o – dog, u – pup.

Give lots of practice with three-letter words.

Teach the child to blend sounds together smoothly in words in reading and printing.

Give enough time and practice with each sound until saying it alone and in words becomes automatic.

The long vowel sounds are a – cake, e – bee, i – kite, o – rope, u – tune. Practice combinations of letters to make words with long vowel sounds ending with the letter e.

Other long vowel sound combinations are ai – pail, ay – day, ea – read, ie – tie, oa – boat, ue – cue.

Teach the child to blend consonant sounds together – bl – blame, br – brag, sl – sleep, st – step, str – street. Give plenty of words for practice.

Make up sentences. You will have to use some sight words. The – The dog is black.

Teach the combinations ch – chap, sh – sheep, th – this, wh – wheel.

Teach g as in badge, c as in dance.

Teach other combinations:

ank – thank, ang – rang, er – her, ar – car, ing – sing,
ea – head, ink – think, ie – field, ei – seize, ey – key, y – fly,
igh – high, ight – night, ou – mouth, ew – new, aw – saw,
or – more, ur – fur, oi – boil, oy – toy, ough – tough, all – ball,
ull – full, tion – station, ain – mountain, ous – joyous.

Teach words of more than one syllable. Each syllable
can be read as easily as a short word: cat – tle – cattle,
ba – na – na – banana, cab – bage – cabbage.

That's all there is to it. There are a few more sounds, which
can be taught in the same way.

Aa	Bb	Cc	Dd	Ee	Ff
Gg	Hh	Ii	Jj	Kk	Ll
Mm	Nn	Oo	Pp	Qq	Rr
Ss	Tt	Uu	Vv	Ww	Xx
Yy	Zz				

a

b	ba
c	ca cab k back
d	da dab cab Dad bad add
f	fa fab fad
g	ga gab gad bag gag
h	ha hack had hag
j	ja jab Jack jag
l	la lab lack lad lag
m	ma Mac mad am dam ham jam Pam
n	na nab an Ann ban can Dan fan man Nan
p	pa pack pad pal pan cap gap lap map nap
q	qua quack
r	ra rack rat rag ram ran rap
s	sack sad sag Sam sap gas lass pass as has
t	ta tab tack tag tam tan tap at bat cat fat hat mat pat rat sat
v	va van vat have
w	wa wag
x	axe fax tax wax
y	ya yak yam
z	zap jazz

Read down

			am	an
back	bad	bag	cab	dam	ban
Jack	Dad	lag	dab	ham	can
lack	fad	nag	gab	jam	Dan
pack	had	rag	lab	Pam	fan
quack	lad	sag	nab	Sam	man
sack	mad	tag	tab	tam	Nan
tack	pad	wag		yam	pan
yak	rad				ran
	sad				van

bat	cap	axe
cat	gap	fax
fat	lap	tax
hat	map	wax
mat	nap	fax
pat	rap	
rat	sap	
sat	tap	
vat	zap	

Read across

cat sap tan dam tab back Dan
Sam tam fad map nab rag lad
nap mat Pam yak quack mad rap
wax jam tag cab gap fat sad tack
ham ban lap gab nag had lack
cap pat ran tap fan hat man bad
fax Dad yam axe bat bag pad
pack rad Jack lag dab rat sag
sat sack wag lab vat van pan

on   At cat sat on a mat.
      Dan has a cap.
      A fat cat sat on Nan's lap.
      Ann has a map.
the   Nan can pat the cat.
      The rat ran.
his   Jack has a pack sack on his back.
in   Sam has ham in the pan.
      Dan can wax the van.

The man has a hat.
Can Nan have the wax?

ch	chap chat batch catch hatch latch match patch
sh	shack shag bash cash dash hash rash
th	thatch thank bath math path than that
wh	whack wham

to	That man ran to catch the cab. A rat ran on the path. Ann can have a bath.

black brag bran brass clam clan clap
class clash crab crash drab drag
flag flat flash glad glass grab
grass plan slab slag slam slap slash
splash track tram trap trash thrash

and ant ask band hand land sand
grand fast last mast blast past stand
mask damp tramp stamp splash plant
gasp clasp grasp ranch branch can't
ank bank sank tank yank blank shank
thank drank prank Frank spank

ang	bang rang sang
g(e)	badge
c(e)	dance chance glance
	Jack has cash in the bank.
	A flag flaps on the mast.
	The yak stands on the sand.
is	A jazz band is on the stand.
	A black bat hangs on the branch.

Adam salad attack jackal dazzle candle baggage banana Alaska Allan Santa canvas atlas castle sample manage bandana Japan panda Grandma Grandpa apple cattle battle cabbage package crabapple Alana Amanda lava language palace saddle rattle bandage flapjack Canada caravan mammal

ed	handed banded landed saddled
es	patches matches ashes
of	The atlas has a map of Canada.
	Alana handed a package to Grandma.

Dan has an apple and a banana.
Adam has cattle at the ranch.

er   after batter fatter hatter matter
       chatter shatter faster master hammer
       lantern hamster banner manner
       panther plaster splatter ladder
       stagger camper badger stammer
       cracker camera salamander
       platter perhaps pattern

her   Nan has a salamander in her hand.
       Japan is a land on the map.
       Pam ran faster than Nan.
       A black panther sat on the grass.
       The glass shattered in the blast.
       The panda has black patches.
       The hamster ran to the cabbage
       patch.

ing   batting patting napping slapping
       trapping grabbing slamming
       flapping planning sagging
       standing smashing crashing
       planting chanting splashing

tramping thanking asking waxing
chattering chatting

The yak is standing on the sand.
Alana is waxing the van.
Pam is planting the cabbage patch.

happy snappy Sally valley Andy
Randy Mandy candy handy
Nancy fancy shaggy carry marry
battery shabby angry fantasy any
anything
Andy and Randy have a bag of candy.

are   The cattle are standing in the valley.
Nancy has a fancy hat.
Mandy can carry the baggage.

e

bed beg ball Ben bet cell deck
den fed fell get gem hem hen
jell jet keg led leg less let
men mess met neck Ned Nell
net peck peg pen pet red
sell set Ted tell ten vet web

well wet yell yes yet egg
here were

ai   said again
ay   says
        Ted fed the pet hens in the pen.
        Sally can sell the eggs.

end   bend lend mend send blend elf
        self best nest pest rest vest
        west belt felt melt bent cent dent
        rent sent tent went desk held
        help kept bench let's Fred smell
        spell dress tenth twelve

        shed shell check chess chest
        then them there when where
        fetch flesh

        better letter wetter pepper letting
        getting wetting smelling spelling
        helping

        very berry cherry penny Betty
        Teddy celery

Betty is spelling very well.
Ann had better send that letter.
Mandy has a cabbage and celery salad.

ea   dead head lead read bread bear
     tear wear year spread thread
     wealth health healthy ready
     instead meant leather weather
     feather sweater

Pam spread jam on the bread.
The red dress has a tear.
Fred read the letter.

ie   friend
ei   their

     enter exam travel present planet
     seven desert dessert kettle settle
     every Texas blanket basket
     camel teddy very magnet celery
     parent extra express satchel
     taxes everything gentle gentleman
     pretty berry twenty shelter nestle
     herself happen velvet several

glasses sentence telegram
vegetable attend attempt cassette
message grandparent address
necessary tragedy calendar
wedding traveller September
camera mending secretary

ph   elephant telegraph alphabet

Dan can tell the letters of the
alphabet.
Fred sent a telegraph message to
his friend at the wedding.
Pam's grandparents travelled to
Texas.

i

if ill in is it bib bid big bill bin
bit Dick did dig dill dim din
dip ditch dish fib fig fill fin fit
fish fix gill give hid him his hit
jig Jill Jim kid kill kin kiss kit
lick lid kip lit live mill mitt
Nick pick pig pill pin pit quick
quill quit rib Rick rid rig rim rip

sick sill sin sit six tick till Tim
tin tip wick wig win witch wish
will wit with chick chill chin
chip ditch rich which thick ship
whip thin thick this

Dick has chip dip in a dish.

brick bridge crib drill frill grill
stick still gift lift milk silk slid slip
ridge skin skip strip click cliff
clip swim shift swift fist hint wind
mist twig twin trip trick prince
drift drip its didn't

ink   ink mink pink rink sink wink blink
brink drink stink

ing   ring sing wing sting bring spring
sting singing stinging winking
drinking sinking fixing mixing
picking swimming skimming
chipping rigging digging

The wind sang in the rigging of the ship.
The fish is swimming with its fins.

bigger himself magic exist rabbit
radish satin spinach river city
giggle fiddle terrible winter
milkman sandwich kitchen finish
kitten silver whimper little
penguin fiddle different plastic
engine wicked practice children
cabin cricket princess middle
taxi fiddler traffic village signal
pickle picnic mitten pencil selfish
dentist zipper insect dinner
napkin signal chicken active
pigpen sister simple whisper
winner dipper minute prison
invent nickel

The little rabbit hid in the cabbage
patch.
The wicked witch hid in the ditch.
In winter, children slid on the hill.
The princess lives in a castle.

interest criminal minister animal
family medicine fantastic
fisherman activity taxicab Africa
America sandwiches accident

Thanksgiving mathematics crystal
physics system sympathy

The animal is a mammal.
Elephants live in Africa.
The criminal went to prison.
The family had sandwiches and
drinks in their picnic basket.
The Sahara desert is in Africa.

o

off of on Bob bog box cob cod
cot dock dog doll Don dot fog
fox gone got hock hog hop hot
job jog jot lock log lot mop not
pop pot rob rock rob rot sob
sock top toss tot chop shock
shop shot shone

Don has gone to the pop shop.
The dog sat on top of the log.

blot block clock cloth crock crop
cross drop flock flop frock frog
froth gloss loft smock smog

stock stop trot bond fond pond
long strong song solve honk

Tick tock said the clock.
The frog swam in the pond.
A thick fog settled on the city.

along above among robin
dolphin common monster closet
robber rocket lemon hockey
problem contest cottage proper
otter oxen object across fossil
omelet goblin carrot pocket
gossip cobweb cotton copper
ribbon canyon lollipop parrot
comic person wagon ostrich
lobster concert Robert cockpit
donkey rocker bottle tonsil soccer
bottom chocolate gallop problem
thermometer democracy

hopped hopping stopped stopping
shopped shopping chopped
chopping rotted rotting spotted
spotting

There are fossils in the rocks in the canyon.
Robert solved a problem in mathematics.
The children attended a concert.

u

up us buck bud bug budge bun but buzz cub cuff cup cut duck dug dull fudge fun fuzz gull gum gun huff hug hull hush hum hut jug judge luck muck mud mug nut much puck puff pup rub rush tuck tug sun such shut chug chum

The bug runs on the rug.
It is fun to run in the sun.

bust bunch brush dust dump crush crunch just must rust stun spun shun hunt grunt bump jump pump junk sunk stung hump lump drug drum thump flush pluck truck snug club plum

clump skunk blush shrunk stump
trump slush shrub shrug cluck
trunk much munch

He is as snug as a bug in a rug.
The dump truck is stuck in the mud.

juggle muffin ugly summer under
juggler hundred puppy bumpy
bathtub bubble thunder supper
number puppet bunny sunny
discuss bubbling puzzle rubber
octopus funny guppy running
topic study umbrella pumpkin
uncle butter drumming until
subtract button shuttle hungry

o

come some from monkey mother
brother front money honey cover
month other won wonder done
does love dove glove something
somewhere coming

ou   double trouble cousin country

Summer is coming and the weather
is getting hotter.
Jack will study until supper

a-e

ace age bake bale base cage
cake came cane cape case cave
Dale date Dave daze face fade
fake fame fate game gate gave
gaze hate haze jade Jake Jane
Kate lace lake lame lane late
made make mate maze name
pace page pale pane pave
quake race rage rake rate sage
sake sale same sane save take
tale tame tape vane vase wade
wage wake wave chase shade
shame shape whale bathe

Jane and Dale bake a cake.
Dave came late to the game.
Kate has the same last name as Dale.
The children race to the gate.

baker maker baking making
taking racing wading naming
taping chasing waking

range change blade Blake blame
blaze brake crane flake flame
frame grade grape graze place
plane plate snake stake stale
state trace trade space spade
haste paste taste bathe

The flame blazed as the wind
picked up.
The space shuttle blasted up at
take-off.

awake amaze pancake lemonade
rattlesnake cavalcade cradle table
salesman April native danger
laziness lazy paper later apron
celebrate estimate able basement
maple baby safety cable

Chocolate cake and lemonade were
on the table.

ai

aid aim bail fail faith Gail gain
jail maid mail main nail paid pail
pain quail raid rain sail tail vain
wait chain

brail brain drain grain plain Spain
stain strain snail trail train faint
paint saint quaint raisin afraid
baler trailer

A snail sat on the trail.
The rain in Spain fell on the plain.
A quaint little village nestled in the
valley.

ay

bay day hay jay lay may pay
ray say way away
ey   they

day gray play pray tray stay
today yesterday crayon railway
playmate subway Sunday Monday

of	The months of April and May come in the spring.
	Today is Sunday, the tenth of May.

ei	eight freight weight weigh neighbor
ea	great break steak

e

be he me we she these

ee

bee see wee beef been beet
beech deed feed feel feet geese
heel jeep keen keep queen
queer peek peep seed seek
seem seen weed week weep
teeth

free freeze sleep sleeve street
fleet sleet sweep sweet greet
green breeze freeze sneeze
sheep sheet cheek cheese creep

cheer creek three coffee toffee
sleepy creepy

ea

ear eat each bead beam bean
beat beach dear deal fear gear
heap hear heat jeans leaf leak
lean leap leave leash meal mean
near neat peas peach read real
rear reach sea seal seam seat
tea tear teach tease cheat cheap
east beast feast least dream
cream breathe please clean clear
creak freak sneak

eagle easy Easter beaver weary
dreary teacher teaches peanut
reading teaching reason measles
nearly clearly dearly reader

Please teach me to read.
Reading is easy.
Pass the cheese, please.
It is late and we feel sleepy.
A bee is buzzing near the tree.

ie	field shield yield niece thief chief grief piece shriek relief believe
ei	receive deceive weird ceiling seize either neither
ey	key

Beavers eat the green leaves of trees. They cut the trees with their teeth. The branches are dragged to make a dam. When they hear danger, they slap their tails on the pond to tell their friends that danger is near. Then they swim to safety.

The man planted a field of wheat. The rain came and the sun shone. Later the heads of wheat waved in the breeze. Bread will be made from the grains of wheat.

recess needle freezer pretend December really became remember evening eleven between meaning request behave

become appear disappear
erupt erase prevent trampoline
responsible beyond fifteen zebra
debate sixteen seventeen effect
geology geography athlete
experience

i

ice bike bite dike dime dine dive
dice file fine five fire hide hive
jive kite like life lime line live
mice mike mile mine nice nine
pike pile pine pipe quite ride rice
ripe side size tide tile time vine
wide wife wine wipe shine whine
while white

Five white mice ate the rice.

for   We will ride the bikes for a mile.

drive price pride prime prize slice
slide slime spine spike swine
tribe twine smile twice

ie	die lie pie tie cried fried died tied tried

| y | by my fly sky try cry shy why dye |

Why does the Big Dipper shine in the sky?

| i | I I'm I'd I'll |

| igh | high sigh sight might right tight light fight night fright bright |

| ei | height |

| ind | bind find kind mind blind mild child |

Please pass me a slice of raisin pie.
I can hear the bees buzzing in the hive.

fly flies cry cries cried try tries tried

The kite flies high in the sky.

fireman violet lion bonfire inside
delight pirate tiger tiny butterfly
beside primary license midnight
July flashlight decide satellite
quiet library pineapple divide
reply lightning Friday giant silent
valentine sometime sunshine
multiply spider environment
identify idle myself digest
dynamite crocodile appetite
bicycle tricycle

o oe

go no so foe Joe toe goes toes
oh o'clock

o-e

bone code cone coke hole home
hope hose lone mole nose note
poke pole quote robe rode rope
rose sole tone vote woke zone
choke chose phone those whole
drove drone slope stone stove

throne stole smoke spoke awoke
broke close clothes

The tiny mole disappeared into his
hole.
He awoke at the smell of smoke.
It was no joke when my bike broke.
The dog hid a bone under the
stone.

oa

boat coat moat coal foal goal
coach load loam loan road roam
soak soap toad

coast toast float throat roast
boast oats

A load of coal went along the road.
The soap made bubbles of foam in
the bathtub.
We like to roam, but it's nice to
come home.
My boat can float.

o   old cold fold hold mold sold told
older colder oldest coldest most
post don't roll

ow

bow bowl low row sow tow blow
flow grow throw show snow crow
own blown flown grown thrown

The winter wind blows the cold
snow.
The plants grow in a row.

crocus open grocery alone follow
hello buffalo donut tadpole robot
golden oatmeal below hollow
flamingo zero window mobile
yellow notice over broken stolen
jello poet volcano envelope
snowflake radio snowman
potato tomato motor explode
spoken bingo soldier shallow
tallow pillow meadow October
November telephone photograph

Hallowe'en jack-o-lantern billow
willow videotape suppose explode
hostess only microwave

There were potatoes and oatmeal in
the groceries.
The volcano erupted and smoke
and ashes billowed into the sky.
A jack-o-lantern sat on the window
sill on Hallowe'en.

ou

mould shoulder boulder though

u-e

use cute cube duke dune tube
tune

ew

new news few pew stew renew

ue

cue due duel fuel

We will hear the news on the radio.
Joe can play a new tune.

Tuesday unite united community
useless nephew newspaper
ambulance eventually January
barbecue computer

ure

picture pasture measure treasure
pleasure capture rapture
temperature

oo

cool coop coon food fool goose
loon loop loot loose mood moon
noon pool roof room poor root
soon too tool zoom gloom groom

stool stoop spoon smooth spook
choose spool zoo

o

do to who shoe lose into whose
whom

kangaroo balloon afternoon
bedroom mushroom baboon
today tonight whoever rooster
booster

ou u

you youth soup fruit wound
through group super superman
supernatural superintendent

Dan threw a stone through the
window.

ue ew ui

blue true blew flew juice fruit

oo

book cook look nook took wood
good shook brook wool foot
cookie goodbye

ou u

could would should journey put
pull push pudding pulling pushing

ow

owl fowl bow cow how now
row sow vow wow clown crowd
crown town down brown flower
tower shower

ou

our out bout pout loud cloud
flour bound found hound loud
mound pound round sound
wound ground mouse house
louse south shout pounce bounce
mouth thousand announce about
around

The brown cow lay down on the
ground.
The clown bowed to the crowd.
A little mouse ran into the house.
Flowers bloom after the summer
showers.

aw

caw jaw paw raw saw straw
dawn fawn crawl lawn pawn
shawl drawn hawk

Dawn saw a crow on the lawn.

au

fault taught caught August pause
cause haul sauce Paul sausage
because daughter restaurant

ou

ought bought fought thought

all

all ball call fall gall hall mall pall
wall small wallet swallow football
baseball

The small ball will fall when it
bounces on the wall.
Don has his wallet in his pocket.

ar

are bar car far jar tar star arch
arm ark art barn farm harm
large barge bark hark lark park

card hard lard yard chart smart
march start

A car drove into the yard at the
farm.
A large barge is on the lake.

car park apartment farmer garden
carpet regard regardless barley
party alarm wizard marmalade
marshmallow supermarket

or

or for nor core more pore sore
tore wore form torn worn score
shore born corn horn storm
chore shore stork cord horse
torch pork porch

The storm tore the leaves from the
trees.

oar oor

boar board door

ar

war warm wart warn warble
quart quarter

our

four pour your mourn courage
tournament fourteen

correct border former boring
tomorrow borrow sorrow forest
forecast popcorn before corner
forlorn important porridge morning
foreman forty tornado history
story horizon order explorer

er

clerk her fern herd perch herself
berth person alert servant perfect
emergency after

ear

earn learn earth early earnest
earthquake heard search
research

ir

fir firm first girl bird stir skirt
shirk birth third swirl circus
birthday squirrel

Dawn had a party for her third
birthday.
The girl has a bird in her hand.

ur

fur purr burn turn churn curl
church burst curve furl turkey
turnip nursery purple Saturday
Thursday hamburger turtle

or

work world worse worm word
homework worry tractor sailor
color mayor tractor

a

wash water walk talk stalk chalk
was want waddle salt father what
also almost always

are

care dare fare mare pare rare
share snare scare square stare

air

air fair hair pair chair

ear

bear pear tear wear year

ian

Canadian Indian Australian

tion

nation station national
construction exhibition invitation
plantation invention position
graduation subscription question
diction dictation dictionary
mention education infection lotion
motion attention

He will renew his subscription to the
newspaper.

Education is necessary in a democracy.
The secretary took dictation.

oi

oil boil coil foil spoil joint point noise voice

The noise at the exhibition drew his attention.

oy

boy Roy royal employ enjoy voyage

Roy read the story of the royal wedding.

sion shion

tension mansion pension
occasion decision vision television
cushion fashion comprehension

They made a decision to close the television station.

ile ine ice

automobile   machine   magazine
police

Don read about machines in the automobile magazine.

ful

full pull wonderful cheerful useful
helpful beautiful

ain

mountain fountain curtain

ous ious

joyous dangerous glamorous
cautious precious delicious

The explorer went on a dangerous journey.

ough

tough rough enough

ough

cough trough

c s

special ocean sugar sure artificial

These words have silent letters.

calf half lamb comb thumb dumb
numb climb answer wrap write written
wrote wrist wrap wrong wring knit
knot know knee knife knives kneel
knock island hymn autumn solemn
debt doubt listen mortgage ghost gnaw
gnome Christmas character school
scheme chemistry science scenery
scissors scene rhyme rhubarb psychic
pneumonia build built spaghetti bruise
cruise laugh naughty two buy business
people eye nuisance aunt Wednesday

The beautiful mountain scenery passed
by the train windows.

They had a delicious meal in the
restaurant.

The mountain climbers were cautious on
the dangerous slope.

Dick played the character of Santa Claus in the Christmas concert at school.

Artificial sweeteners are sometimes used in foods instead of sugar.

Jan read the chemistry section in the science magazine.

They admired the beautiful autumn leaves.

The children enjoyed the ocean cruise.

People who have learned to sound words can read books, magazines, and newspapers.

Printed in the United States
By Bookmasters